Spike the spy

Written by Abigail Steel

Illustrated by Alex Patrick

RISING ★ STARS

Then they went to visit Mike.

He will be waiting for us.

Mike lived at flat number nine.

Chime! Chime!

Come inside!

Mike gave Spike and Dad some pie.

But Spike spotted that Mike was sad.

Mike began to cry.

His cat had not been seen for days.

Spike felt bad for Mike.

What can we do?

Mike had tried to find her.

I just wish I had better legs!

Dad helped to make a plan.

They set off to find Bella.

Spike and Dad went to the park.

They peeked behind the trees.

Next, they tried the road behind the shops.

But Bella was not there.

Spike felt upset.

I hope she was not taken by a thief.

They set off for Mike's flat.

He will be so sad.

Just then, Spike spotted a black tail.

They stopped and looked.

Dad called across the garden.

It was Bella!

Bella had a collar on.

Look at her tag!

Bella

Thank you!

Bella went on
a little holiday!

Spike handed Bella back to Mike.

Bella had liked her holiday!

Mike kept smiling at Bella.

Thank you, Spike.

Spike smiled, too.

I liked being Spike the Spy!

Talk about the story

Answer the questions:

1 What number flat did Mike live at?

2 Why couldn't Mike look for Bella?

3 How did Spike and his dad find Bella?

4 Why do you think Spike liked being 'Spike the Spy'?

5 Have you ever gone looking for something that was lost? What happened?

6 Would you like to be a spy? Why or why not?

Can you retell the story in your own words?